To William

Happy Christmas 2011

Love
Nana + Bill
xx

A child's first 123

COUNTING

Alison Jay

templar publishing

1 one little girl sleeping

2 two soaring wings

3 three
little pigs

4 four frog princes

5 five fluffy ducklings

6 six gingerbread men

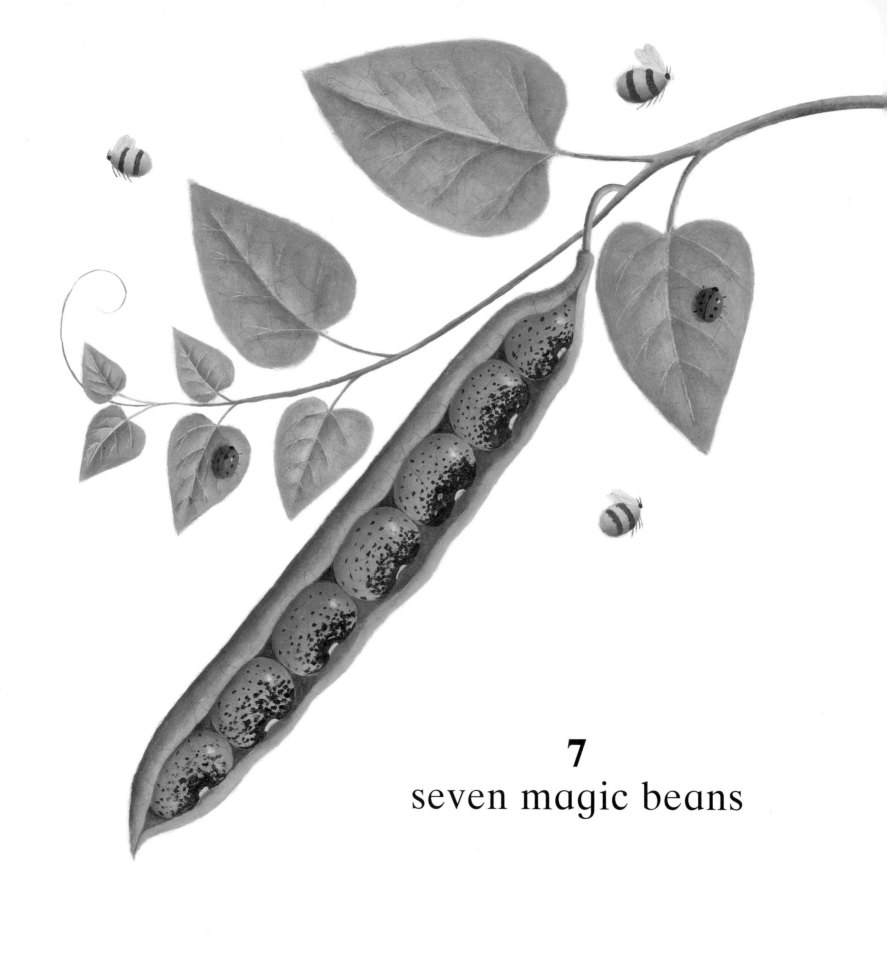

7
seven magic beans

THE PALACE · HAMELIN TOWN

ENCHANTED FOREST

8 eight running rats

9
nine golden eggs

10 ten
sharp
teeth

9
nine perfect roses

8
eight fancy
footmen

7 seven
marching dwarves

6 six shiny sweets

5 five fluttering fairies

4 four royal mattresses

3 three angry bears

2 two dancing shoes

1 one little
girl waking...

DID YOU RECOGNISE THE FAIRYTALE?

THE THREE LITTLE PIGS

THE FROG PRINCE

THE UGLY DUCKLING

THE GINGERBREAD MAN

JACK AND THE BEANSTALK

THE PIED PIPER of HAMELIN

THE GOOSE THAT LAID A GOLDEN EGG

LITTLE RED RIDING HOOD

BEAUTY AND THE BEAST

CINDERELLA

SNOW WHITE AND THE SEVEN DWARVES

HANSEL AND GRETEL

SLEEPING BEAUTY

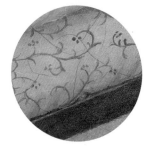

THE PRINCESS AND THE PEA

GOLDILOCKS AND THE THREE BEARS

THE RED SHOES

FOR ALISON B,
HAPPY COUNTING —
ALISON J

A TEMPLAR BOOK
First published in the UK in 2007 by Templar Publishing
www.templarco.co.uk

Illustration copyright © 2007 by Alison Jay
Text and design copyright © 2007 by The Templar Company plc

First edition

ISBN: 978-1-84011-464-5

Designed by Janie Louise Hunt • Concept by Stella Gurney • Edited by Libby Hamilton

Printed in China